Y0-DKB-068

Moose

Amazing Photos & Fun Facts Book About Moose For Kids

Remember Me Series

By

Caroline Norsk

Copyright © 2014 by Caroline Norsk

All rights reserved. No part of this book may be used or reproduced in any manner whatsoever without the express written permission of the publisher except for the use of brief quotations in a book review

Image Credits: Royalty free images reproduced under license from various stock image repositories. Under a creative commons licenses.

Remember me I am a moose.

Remember me I am a mammal.

Remember me I have very long and thin legs.

Remember me I am the largest among the deer family.

Remember me I like to live in cold places.

Remember me I have very huge antlers on my head.

Remember me in some places I am called an elk.

Remember me I love to eat plants and fruits.

Remember me I am a good swimmer.

Remember me a male moose has antlers.

Remember me I use my legs to walk through snow.

Remember me I can usually be found alone in the woods.

Remember me I use my antlers to defend myself.

Remember me I can be seen usually in Canada and Alaska.

Remember me I can sometimes eat the bark of a tree when I am hungry.

Remember me I use my antlers to fight another moose.

Remember me the ones that come after me are bears and wolves.

Remember me I am a very large animal.

Remember me I can have a mean temper.

Remember me my antlers grow along with me.

Thank you.

Good Luck.

62898837R00015

Made in the USA
Lexington, KY
21 April 2017